New York

ARCHITECTURE IN DETAIL

New York

MARCIA REISS

PRC

Dedication: To Charlie, Julie, and Peter
for your advice, support, and inspiration.

Acknowledgments: Thanks to Simon Clay for the wonderful pho-
tographs, to Ray Gastil, Kyle Johnson, and Carol Clark for great
suggestions, and to the many others who provided essential help
and information: Deborah Bershad, New York City Art
Commission; Lauren Daniluk, New 42nd Street, Inc.; Norma
Foederer, Mike Keane, and Nancy Lara, Trump Organization;
Scott Glaser, U.S. Custom House; Liz Pearson, New York Public
Library; Patrick Pleven, New York City Film Office; Alan Ritchie;
Philip Johnson & Alan Ritchie; Tinoa Rodgers, Riverside Church;
Robert Russo, Madison Square Garden/Radio City Music Hall;
and Nanette Smith, New York City Mayor's Office.

Bibliographical References:
Dolkart, Andrew S., *Guide to New York City Landmarks*, John
Wiley & Sons, Inc., 1998.
Goldberger, Paul, *The Skyscraper*, Alfred A. Knopf, 1989.
Stern, Robert A. M. and others, *New York 1880; New York
1960*, The Monacelli Press, 1997–1999.
New York 1900; New York 1930, Rizzoli International
Publications, 1987-1992.
White, Norval and Willensky, Elliot, *AIA Guide to New York City*,
Three Rivers Press, 2000.
Wolfe, Gerard R., *New York: A Guide to the Metropolis*, Mc-Graw
Hill, Inc., 1994.

Produced 2003 by
PRC Publishing Ltd,
64 Brewery Road, London N7 9NT
A member of **Chrysalis** Books plc

This edition published 2003
Distributed in the U.S. and Canada by:
Sterling Publishing Co., Inc.
387 Park Avenue South, New York, NY 10016

© 2003 PRC Publishing Ltd

ISBN 1 85648 667 2

Printed and bound in Malaysia

Photo acknowledgments:
The publisher wishes to thank Simon Clay for taking all the photography in this book, and Marcia Reiss for her help in arranging
the photo shoot. Additional thanks to the staff at the Custom
House, and to all those who kindly gave their permission for pho-
tography to be taken on their premises. With the exception of
the images listed below, all photography is copyright © Chrysalis
Images:
Page 94: © Rod Mickens/American Museum of Natural History
and Page 95: © D. Finnin/American Museum of Natural History.
Front cover shows: the Guggenheim Museum interior (©
Chrysalis Images, see pages 72–75 for further details).
Back cover shows: the Flatiron Building (© Chrysalis Images, see
pages 32–35 for further details).
Page 1: Grand Central Terminal Clock and page 2: The
Woolworth Building.

Contents

Introduction

New York City is a universe of famous buildings. Constellations of dazzling structures have burst onto the city skyline during different eras of architectural brilliance. The slender island of Manhattan, the smallest in area yet most intensely developed part of the city, has more buildings per square foot than any other American city.

To chose any group of famous New York buildings inevitably leaves many others out. Each of the twenty featured in this book is extraordinary in its own right and, at the same time, is a significant chapter in the city's history. From the colonial era through the development of the skyscraper to today's world of high-tech design, they are milestones in the evolution of New York. To read their stories is to discover the fast-forward world of finance, fashion, politics, and the powerful personalities that shaped the city—and the state of urban architecture—over the past two centuries.

The builders and architects of New York make up a star-studded roster of famous and fascinating individuals. Yet no single personality has been able to put his or her stamp on this dynamic city and make it stick. Manhattan's long finger of land has pointed the way to prominence, pushing up development, and molding neighborhoods along its entire length. But the limits of the island itself, only two miles wide and thirteen miles long, created a fierce competition for building sites. Just a year after the end of the Civil War, in the midst of a furious pace of new construction, the New York diarist George Templeton Strong noted that "a new town has been built on top of the old one and another excavated under it." His observation has been true ever since. Constantly rebuilding and reinventing itself, New York has been a perpetual motion machine of innovation and change.

Right: Close in location but a world apart in architectural styles are the Chrysler Building (1930, William Van Alen), right, and the United Nations Plaza Hotel (1976, Roche Dinkeloo Associates), left.

Since the city began at the southern tip of Manhattan, the chronology of its development follows its geography, unfolding from south to north, or as New Yorkers say, from downtown to uptown. *Architecture in Detail: New York* begins with the oldest and smallest church still standing in Manhattan, St. Paul's Chapel. Deep within downtown's skyscraper canyons, this colonial-era chapel was suddenly thrust into new service as a rescue center when the World Trade Center towers collapsed across the street. St. Paul's is only one of many remarkable buildings cast in a new light by the loss of the towers. Even some of the city's icons, such as the Empire State Building, had been taken for granted until tragedy sharpened the focus on their importance. Other distinctive structures often miss the attention they deserve simply because they have been a constant presence in everyday life, such as graceful City Hall, dutifully carrying out the city's business for two centuries. Whether long-time favorites, high-tech newcomers, or hidden treasures, all twenty buildings deserve a closer look.

Through the first half of the nineteenth century, the New York skyline, like the profile of a medieval city, was no higher than its church spires. St. Paul's Chapel was the city's tallest building from 1796 to 1846, the year its parent, Trinity Church, was rebuilt and took all the glory. Even the mini-palatial City Hall (1811), allowed houses of worship to rule the heavens. Troops of commercial buildings marched up the skyline in the second half of the century, yet the tallest

structure built in this period was not a building at all, but the Brooklyn Bridge, the world's greatest construction project of the century. As the bridge towers rose in the 1870s, they surpassed the height and scale of every building in the city. At the same time, the foundation for other monumental structures was also being laid.

While world capitals rose to power as centers of religion or politics, New York was built on commerce. Seizing on the city's strategic location as a port, government and business leaders ringed Manhattan with new docks and rail lines after the Civil War. By the start of the twentieth century, imposing buildings such as the U.S. Custom House (1907) and Grand Central Terminal (1913) proclaimed New York's leading role in trade and commerce.

When the leaders of this era built monuments to their success, they looked to Europe for style and authenticity. Intentionally or not, their buildings also reflected the city's polyglot

Far Left: This sweeping view of East Midtown illustrates the evolution of architectural glass, from the United Nations Secretariat tower, left, the city's first example of a glass curtain wall, to the taut folds of glass enveloping the United Nations Plaza buildings, right (1976–1983, Roche Dinkeloo Associates). To the far right is the Chrysler Building, from an earlier age of brick and steel construction.

Left: Now dwarfed by modern skyscrapers, St. Paul's was Manhattan's tallest tower through the first half of the nineteenth century.

population. Taken for granted today, the city's cosmopolitanism was another product of its commercial success, which attracted millions of immigrants to the land of opportunity. In 1898, the year Manhattan joined with the other four boroughs to form Greater New York City, half of its population was foreign born. Like this multicultural mix, the city's buildings were an exuberant expression of every European style.

But New York soon made its own mark. Forged by the perfection of high-speed elevators and steel construction in the late nineteenth century, the skyscraper revolutionized architecture and gave New York a new symbol of its financial power. After the turn of the century, the New York skyline began to look like no other in the world. Like the glaciers that shaped Manhattan's rocky escarpment, skyscrapers spread from one end of the island to the other, carving out new mountain ranges of buildings.

These towering buildings changed the character of entire neighborhoods. In 1903, the Flatiron Building rose on 23rd Street and Fifth Avenue like the prow of a ship leading development into new waters beyond Lower Manhattan. A generation before, the site had been a fashionable residential area where people such as the novelist Edith Wharton were born into elite society. While the rich kept moving uptown, commercial buildings became as important as churches and imitated their styles. Soaring with Gothic splendor, the Woolworth Building (1913) became the "Cathedral of Commerce." In turn, houses of worship imitated commercial buildings, culminating in the ultimate skyscraper church. At twenty-four stories, Riverside Church (1930) was taller than the Flatiron Building.

As unbridled economic forces led to raging development, producing everything from the sky-scraper to the tenement, civic leaders at times placed a temperate, beneficent hand on the city's growth. By the start of the twentieth century, classic public buildings such as the American Museum of Natural History (1877–1924) and the New York Public Library (1911) also had taken shape. Palatial but not intimidating, their vast corridors and vaulted rooms were as generous as their goals of serving the public.

Great buildings changed the face of the city and extended its commercial frontiers. The Library came to 42nd Street after another Beaux-Arts building, Grand Central Terminal, had built a city within a city on top of its expanded railroad tracks. The immense project turned New York's northern outskirts into Midtown, a new office district that rivaled Wall Street as the skyscraper kingdom. In the 1920s, the Chrysler Building, a vision of fantasy—one with a competitive streak—was one of dozens of skyscrapers racing to become the tallest in the world. In 1931, the Empire State Building became king of the sky-line, just as the Depression brought the race to a screeching halt.

The Rockefellers carried a large part of the city's construction industry through the Depression by building Rockefeller Center and Radio City Music Hall (1932–1940). The

Left: The towers of the Brooklyn Bridge were the city's first skyscrapers, rising higher and plunging deeper into Manhattan's bedrock foundation than any other structure had done before.

Right: Once the world's tallest building, the Woolworth is still one of the city's most distinctive skyscrapers.

enormous complex startled critics with its unprecedented size, but would later be recognized for its sophisticated urban design.

The economic resurgence after World War II brought architects of legendary fame and innovation to New York. Le Corbusier's concept for the United Nations Headquarters (1953) was the city's first glass curtain wall, a type of construction that changed the face of modern architecture. Frank Lloyd Wright's spiral-shaped Guggenheim Museum (1959) broke with tradition on elegant Fifth Avenue, weaving bold new threads—some said rips—in the city's urban fabric. Advances in steel and glass technology brought more daring newcomers to the city's most fashionable streets. The Lever House (1952) and Mies van der Rohe's Seagram Building (1958) changed Park Avenue from an uninterrupted line of masonry buildings to a glass showcase of corporate towers. New to the city, many corporations such as Lever and Seagram came to New York to establish impressive headquarters and polish their national image. In the process, their buildings took on civic responsibilities, setting a precedent for public plazas as an essential feature of new towers.

As the postwar building boom exploded on the scene, it shattered many monuments of the city's past. Magnificent Penn Station was destroyed in 1963 for a mediocre replacement and

Grand Central Terminal was threatened with the same fate. But after more than a century of brash commercialism and a carefree disregard

Left: The Main Reading Room of the New York Public Library, a magnificent sanctuary in a classical temple of books.

Right: Rockefeller Center, a massive complex of towering office buildings, expansive theaters, rooftop gardens, and underground shops, was the city's largest private real estate venture.

Right: With its sloped roof and aluminum skin, the Citicorp Center was a high-tech newcomer to the New York skyline.

for history, New York finally took time to recognize what it had lost. In 1965, the city made historic preservation a matter of law, protecting Grand Central and many other treasures such as City Hall and St. Paul's Chapel. In years to come, even skyscrapers, not only the historic Woolworth Building and towering Empire State, but also the avant-garde Chrysler, Lever, and Seagram, were designated historic landmarks and preserved for future generations.

The 1960s were also a time when the city took stock of its mistakes in architectural design and urban planning. Well-intentioned innovations had led to unexpected abuses. Anonymous glass towers, barren plazas, and superblock developments were being built at an inhuman scale. The Ford Foundation Building (1967) was one of the first new buildings to take a stand for a better environment. Its lush garden atrium was almost as high as the building, giving office workers a green respite from air-conditioned isolation and artificial lighting. While the Citicorp Center (1977) was built at a colossal scale, its public concourse reached a new level of urban vitality and its distinctive sloped roof was a striking addition to the skyline. Acrobatically balanced on supercolumns, the fifty-nine story tower had a hidden weakness that was discovered a year after it was built. The structural fault was quickly and secretly corrected, a tale as exciting as the tower's daring form.

Although New York developers always seemed to be reaching for the sky, bigger was not always better. Above a certain height, the added costs of deeper foundations and more room for elevator shafts often exceeded economic returns. But to skyscraper developers throughout the twentieth century, from Walter Chrysler to the Rockefellers or Donald Trump, personal monuments were just as important—if not more so—than profits. Trump, the quintessential developer of the extravagant 1980s, cast his name in gold on Trump Tower (1983), an innovative glass box that made a bold entrance on exclusive Fifth Avenue.

The city celebrated its own flamboyancy in the 1990s by undertaking a complete revitalization of Times Square and the Broadway theater district. The transformation from sleaze to vibrant theatricality is brilliantly embodied in the high-tech, flashing facade of the New 42nd Street Studios. The newest and least known of the twenty buildings, this relatively small edifice broke new architectural ground in the first year of the new millennium. Using light as a design element, the architects turned a physical structure into a kinetic form.

With few exceptions, New York's best-known buildings are also its tallest, the kind of structures that always generated both awe and alarm. Throughout the city's history, every big building replaced a smaller one, leading to the nation's most densely developed—and crowded—metropolis. New Yorkers have been decrying buildings that steal light and air for more than a century, just as they have taken enormous pride in their towering skyline. While zoning regulations enacted in 1916 and 1961 changed their shape, the towers kept rising, reaching new heights with the World Trade Center in 1972.

In every era, buildings not only reflected the times, but also changed the way citizens perceived their city. After the roaring 1920s slammed into the stock market crash, novelist F. Scott Fitzgerald went to the top of the new Empire State Building. Looking out at the city's flat edges, he realized with despair that "New York City had its limits and was not a universe in itself after all." Approaching a new millennium with hope and apprehension, New Yorkers also began to look beyond their city. No building better represents the dawning age than the Rose Center for Earth and Space, the new planetarium at the Museum of Natural History. Unveiled in early 2000, this huge sphere within a glass cube is an unblinking eye on the global environment and the unknown future.

To many New Yorkers, the city will never be the same without the World Trade Center towers. As the city ponders the best way to fill the gap in its skyline, critics are beginning to remind us that when the towers came on the scene, they were seen as colossal intruders. Large or small, many of New York's most famous buildings often met with scorn. While different in every conceivable way, the Guggenheim Museum and Trump Tower were both treated as unwelcome additions to Fifth Avenue. Even the fabulous Chrysler Building and urbane Rockefeller Center were at first vilified by critics. Yet over time, the public has had the last word, embracing all of these amazing buildings as its own.

St. Paul's Chapel

Architect: unknown; tower and steeple, 1796, James C. Lawrence

Built: 1764–1796

Walking into the small, serene sanctuary, one finds it hard to imagine that St. Paul's, the oldest church still standing in Manhattan, has survived the city's greatest tragedy. Freshly painted since September 11, 2001, the milk-white columns, pink walls, and pale blue ceiling preserve the simple beauty of the finest colonial interiors. A closer look at the wooden pews reveals scuff marks left by the heavy boots and belts of rescue workers who rested on these benches in the months following the terrorist attacks. Purposely left as "sacramental marks," the scratches are testimony to the chapel's use as a respite center for thousands of volunteers who poured through the mountains of debris across the street, searching for victims of the World Trade Center collapse.

The twin towers once stood directly opposite St. Paul's, soaring above the graceful chapel and its quiet graveyard. The slender steeple now has an ashen cast, but the church—a perfect Georgian building—and even the weathered gravestones still stand as they have for nearly two and a half centuries, unscathed by history.

The Trade Center tragedy was not the first disaster that nearly engulfed St. Paul's. In September 1776, the third month of the Revolutionary War, while the British occupied New York City, a fire, most likely set by

Left: St. Paul's is Manhattan's oldest public building in continuous use. The twin towers once stood directly across the street from the chapel, in the empty space shown behind the steeple.

Right: Although most of the names of the architects of St. Paul's are lost to history, its graceful interior and this starburst pulpit are thought to be the design of Pierre L'Enfant, the creator of the design plan for Washington D.C.

American rebels, consumed 500 buildings in Lower Manhattan—a third of the city. Among the losses was the original Trinity Church a few blocks south of St. Paul's. The chapel, just ten years old, survived the conflagration and went on to become one of the nation's most historic sites, the scene of America's transformation from colony to republic.

The British built the first Trinity Church in 1698 and St. Paul's Chapel in 1766 as the center of the Anglican Church in New York. Modeled on St. Martin's-in-the-Field near London's Trafalgar Square, St. Paul's was the colonial expression of a British masterpiece. Prince William of Orange, later King William IV, worshipped at St. Paul's, as did Lords Cornwallis and Howe, who led major battles against the Americans during the Revolutionary War.

On April 30, 1789, after George Washington took the oath of office a few blocks away, the new president and members of Congress came to St. Paul's to offer their prayers for the young republic. The president continued to worship in the chapel during the brief period when New York City was the nation's capital, and the original seal of the United States still hangs on the wall behind the president's pew.

Once St. Paul's tower was built in 1796, its spire became the tallest feature of the Lower Manhattan skyline and kept that distinction until 1846 when Trinity Church was rebuilt as a grand Gothic Revival edifice. St. Paul's, a branch of Trinity parish, lost its prominence and was also over-shadowed by commercial development that swallowed nearly everything around it in the second half of the nineteenth century. By 1850, St. Paul's imposing Ionic portico looked out on Barnum's

Museum across Broadway and nearly rubbed shoulders along Vesey Street with the Astor House, the leading hotel of the day. By the mid-1870s, virtually all of Manhattan below 14th Street was given over to manufacturing, commerce, and tenements. No street changed more than Broadway, which, an observer noted, "was always being built but never finished."

Throughout the twentieth century, when skyscrapers dwarfed St. Paul's, it never lost its purpose. Today, it is Manhattan's oldest public building in continuous use—never more so than after September 11th when the chapel was open twenty-four hours a day throughout the nine-month rescue operation. At the same time, the chapel resumed its regular religious services only seven weeks after the disaster.

Built of locally quarried stone known as Manhattan schist, St. Paul's is truly part of New York City's bedrock foundation and part of the land itself. Its interior columns are filled with solid oak tree trunks that grew on Manhattan's soil when it was covered with forests. Not long after the chapel was built, the land to the west, where two centuries later the trade towers would rise, became a rough neighborhood of taverns and brothels, ironically called "the Holy Ground." Today,

the name resonates with tragic overtones for the nearly 3,000 trade center victims who perished on this ground. After so much loss, its beauty and tradition are all the more important. Made of the stuff of history, it has taken on new purpose and meaning as a sacred place, rising out of the dust to embody the city's spiritual recovery.

Left: The beautiful interior has been repainted since September 11, but the pews still bear the scuff marks left by the boots and belts of rescue workers who rested here. The scratches were purposely left as "sacramental marks." In this view, the sanctuary is decorated with exhibits commemorating the nine-month rescue and salvage operation.

Right: Modeled on St. Martin's-in-the-Field in London, St. Paul's was the colonial expression of a British masterpiece.

City Hall

Architects: Joseph Francois Mangin and John McComb Jr.

Built: 1802–1811

In a city as large and powerful as New York, it seems surprising that this small, elegant building is still the center of government. The French Renaissance mini-palace is not a mere showplace. New York City's mayor and City Council members are still conducting the city's daily business here as they have done for nearly two centuries. Despite destructive fires, severe deterioration, calls for demolition, grand expansion plans, and waves of political demonstrations at its front door, City Hall has stayed in its original location. Restored several times, it is the same size and in the same wonderful shape as the day it opened in 1811.

Colonial officials governed New York from a tavern near the waterfront and later at Wall Street where the Continental Congress met in 1785. The city fathers wanted a new city hall that would embody New York's aspirations, a mix of European tradition with a fresh American style. In 1802, the city chose a team of two architects. The principal designer was Joseph Francois Mangin, a Frenchman who had worked on the Place de la Concorde, Paris, and John McComb Jr., New York City's first native-born architect, who managed construction and balanced French opulence with Federal simplicity.

Right: City Hall is a combination of French elegance and Federal simplicity. Modern in its day, the Federal style emphasized harmonious proportion. The limestone exterior was applied in the 1950s to replace the peeling marble original.

Far Right: Just inside the front door, a striking pair of self-supporting staircases embraces the central rotunda and curves up toward a magnificent dome.

True to its classical form, the building was encased in white marble. However, only brownstone covered the building's back. The cheaper stone was good enough, it was thought, because the back faced the city's northern outskirts and "would be out of sight to all the world for years to come." By the mid-nineteenth century, New York had spread considerably north of City Hall but city officials decided to stay put, close to Wall Street's financial center. Several plans for annexes were drawn, including an elaborate scheme in 1888 for a pair of seven-story pavilions, one on each side of City Hall, and a bell tower soaring behind it. Fortunately, none of the plans took actual shape, but the condition of the once elegant building was neglected and became "an offence to the sight of the community."

Efforts to demolish City Hall reached a peak of activity in 1893 when an architectural competition was held to design its replacement. The idea of a new, larger building made sense at this time since residents were to vote the next year on the consolidation of all five boroughs into Greater New York City. But old City Hall had some new champions. While Manhattan alone was growing to unprecedented size, tearing down old buildings and erecting ever-larger ones, a group of old guard New Yorkers took a stand against the tide that was washing away the city's history.

A preeminent architect, Charles McKim, had led the way years before by proclaiming City Hall "the most admirable public building in the city." In one of the city's earliest historic preservation campaigns, the Sons of the American Revolution and other blueblood organizations convinced city officials that demolishing City Hall would be "not only a municipal calamity, but an act of vandalism."

The growing government found plenty of room to expand in the towering Municipal Building, designed by McKim, Mead, and White, and completed across the street from City Hall in 1914. (Charles McKim, aging and skeptical of skyscrapers, had little to do with the design.) Three years later, a fire nearly destroyed City Hall's cupola and copper dome, which were later restored to their original appearance.

Eroding for decades, the building's marble exterior was finally replaced in 1954–1956 by limestone, and, this time, the white façade also covered the building's brownstone back. The interior, including several extraordinary meeting rooms, has been restored in recent years.

The graceful, refined building has been an incongruous place for New York City's rough and tumble politics. Over the centuries, legions of protestors have gathered in front of the main entrance, even flooding into the building at times of great unrest. City Hall has always been the place to confront government leaders and capture public attention. Countless groups have done so, including: unemployed workers demanding jobs during the frequent financial panics of the nineteenth century; soldiers' wives pleading for public relief during the Civil War; and construction workers raising an American flag on top of the building in response to the Vietnam War protests.

At the same time, City Hall has been the stately setting for solemn and joyous civic occasions. In 1865, the white building was covered in black drapery and a huge banner with a simple message, "The Nation Mourns," hung over the entrance, as the body of Abraham Lincoln lay in state in the rotunda. Tens of thousands of New Yorkers filled the streets to pay their respects to the slain president, just as others did to celebrate the opening of the Erie Canal in 1825, to welcome Charles Lindbergh in 1927, and to hail the baseball champion Yankees and Mets in more recent times. Throughout its history, City Hall has been a unique landmark, an architectural treasure at the nerve center of the city.

Left: George Washington used this desk in 1789, when New York City was the nation's capital, a brief period more than two decades before City Hall was built. The desk is on display in City Hall's Governor's Room.

Right: The statue on top of the cupola was installed in 1887 as the third version of Justice. The first, a carved wooden figure, was destroyed in a raging fire in 1858. The second, also wood, eventually rotted after a quarter of a century. The current figure is made of copper, but was painted to match the building. The theme of the statue reflects City Hall's early days when it housed the courts as well as every other government office.

Brooklyn Bridge

Engineers: John and Washington Roebling

Built: 1869–1883

In the literal sense of the word, the Brooklyn Bridge was New York City's greatest building of its time—a mighty construction project that surpassed everything architects and engineers had achieved or even imagined. Its towers were the city's first skyscrapers, rising higher and plunging deeper into bedrock than any other structure had done before. Its span was longer than any other in the world. Its cables were spun from steel, a material still new in the mid-nineteenth century. It took fourteen years and sixteen million dollars to complete, three times the original estimates, and more than any other single endeavor of the day. When it opened, it changed the way New Yorkers looked at the city and challenged everything they thought was impossible.

The Brooklyn Bridge was the vision of an extraordinary man, a German engineer who also studied philosophy with Hegel and believed in the power of self-realization. John Augustus Roebling came to the United States in 1831, began manufacturing wire rope, and in 1855, when his design for a railway suspension bridge over Niagara Falls was realized, became known as the best bridge designer in America. He first proposed a bridge over the East River between Manhattan and Brooklyn in 1857. The idea was daunting, but hardly new. Developed in Europe,

Left: The Brooklyn Bridge has inspired generations of poets and painters, from Walt Whitman to Georgia O'Keeffe.

Right: The cables led to some of the greatest problems. After miles of wire had been strung between the towers, frayed ends and other deficiencies were discovered. Fortunately, Roebling had specified wire six times stronger than was actually required.

the modern suspension bridge, consisting of wire cables strung between two towers, and supporting a deck, had been invented in the United States in 1801. Other visionaries had proposed an East River span as early as 1802. One had even recommended a tunnel in the 1830s. But Roebling was the first to offer a practical method of construction and to present it with unwavering certainty and will.

Although an economic panic gripped the city in 1857, Roebling pursued his vision for another decade until the time was right to undertake the massive project. Delayed at first by the Civil War, the bridge was advanced by the postwar boom, enabling New York and Brooklyn, then independent cities, to sell bonds for the project. The weather was also an important factor in convincing government officials to proceed. Ferry service on the East River had always been problematic in winter when ice clogged the slips, and high winds and waves made the crossing slow and hazardous. But the brutally cold winter of 1866 to 1867 created unusually long delays, shutting down the service for weeks at a time, and increasing public demand for the bridge. In spring 1867, the state legislature passed a bill authorizing a private company to begin construction. In his report that year to the company, Roebling proclaimed that the design "will not only be the greatest bridge in existence, but it will be the greatest engineering work of this continent. Its towers...will be ranked as national monuments." Seemingly immodest, his words were prophetic, but he would not live to see his prophecy come true.

In June 1869, just as the final approvals for the bridge had been cleared, Roebling was gravely injured while trying to determine the exact location for the Brooklyn tower. As he stood on the wharf, a ferry rammed the pier, crushing his foot. The wound became infected with tetanus, leading to lockjaw and death a few weeks later. Despite the tragedy, the project continued under the direction of his son, Washington Roebling, an engineer who had built bridges for the Union Army and recently returned from Europe where he had studied the method for sinking the bridge towers in the river. However, this method, excavating under water with pneumatic caissons, would leave him and many others involved in the project, crippled by disease.

The caissons were immense, airtight boxes lowered into the river. Through a system of air and water locks, compressed air was pumped in, forcing out the water and allowing workers to enter and dig out the foundation for the towers. But when they left the compressed atmosphere too quickly, many suffered severe cramps, known as the bends. The condition, caused by nitrogen bubbles trapped in the blood, led to extreme pain and sometimes death. Washington Roebling was stricken in 1872 and was to remain an invalid. His wife, Emily, became his emissary, enabling him to direct construction from his Brooklyn home for the next eleven years.

The base of the Brooklyn tower reached forty-four feet below the riverbed, but the workers had to dig down seventy-eight feet before reaching a stable foundation on the Manhattan side. The towers, rising more than 276 feet above high water, were completed in 1876, promising even greater achievements in the nation's second century. But enormous challenges lay ahead. The approaches to the bridge were nearly as long as the 1595-foot-span between the towers. The path for these granite and limestone roadways had to be cleared on both sides of the river by acquiring and demolishing blocks of homes, shops, and even churches. Massive stone anchorages, as big as buildings themselves, had to be constructed on land behind each tower to hold down the tautly wound cables supporting the span.

From year to year, delays, cost overruns, and corruption scandals took their toll in public and political support. But when the bridge finally opened in 1883, it was universally hailed as a wonder of the world. And it kept up with unforeseen advances into the next century. Crossing on cable cars and horse-drawn trolleys, nineteenth-century New Yorkers could not have imagined how the bridge would prove adaptable to modern transportation. For the first seventy years of its life, the bridge required only routine maintenance. In 1953, the electric trolley tracks were removed and the deck was strengthened to bear the weight of increased motor traffic.

Driving over the bridge today, most New Yorkers are no longer impressed by transportation advances or the length of the span, surpassed by many others. It is the beauty of the structure that captures the imagination. The stone towers, offset by the airy, diagonal web of steel, have inspired many poets and painters. Practical and poetic, the bridge still stirs the city's soul.

U.S. Custom House

Architect: Cass Gilbert; principal sculptor, Daniel Chester French

Built: 1899–1907

When it was completed in 1907, this imposing structure left no doubt in anyone's mind that New York was America's premier port city. Covering three blocks at the foot of Broadway, the seven-story building looked out on Bowling Green, the center of New York's shipping empire, with a bold, three-dimensional façade. Forty-four grand columns, each topped by the head of Mercury, twelve heroic statues representing seafaring powers, and massive figures symbolizing the four continents proudly announced the city's place as America's seat of trade and commerce.

Today, with the port of New York centered in New Jersey, the Custom House presents a different face to Lower Broadway. Although its façade is just as grand as it always was, banners flying above the main entrance now announce the building as the home of the National Museum of the American Indian. The story of this transformation is a study in dramatic change, both in the port and in America's social history.

Perfectly positioned for trade by its geography, New York City realized its potential after the Civil War by building an extensive system of docks and rail lines around Manhattan's shore. These were the days before income tax, when government collected its greatest revenues from customs duties. As the nation's center of trade, New York pulled in the lion's share. Before the war,

Far right: The Custom House is the city's most imposing Beaux-Arts building and an extraordinary expression of civic grandeur. "It is a great Government building," its architect Cass Gilbert said, one that "should express...the wealth and luxury of the great Port of New York...and have a dignity appropriate to a notable public monument."

Right: Detail of the coffered ceiling in the main lobby of the Custom House.

the largest and most lavishly decorated public buildings were dedicated to religion and commerce. In the postwar boom, this also applied to government buildings and the U.S. Custom House was a prime example of civic grandeur.

The building established the reputation of its architect, Cass Gilbert, a Minnesota native who went on to design such prominent landmarks as the Woolworth Building in New York City, the world's tallest skyscraper for many years, and the Supreme Court building in Washington, D.C. The Custom House attracted leading artists such as Daniel Chester French, the sculptor of the "Four Continents" and later creator of the figure of Abraham Lincoln in the Lincoln Memorial, Washington.

Gilbert won the Custom House commission through a design competition with major architectural firms. His closest competitor was Carrere & Hastings, a prominent firm that had just captured the commission for the main branch of the New York Public Library. Both firms proposed a Beaux-Arts design, the classical form established by the Ecole des Beaux Arts in Paris and the style of choice for civic buildings at the turn of the century. Gilbert impressed the jury with a bolder design that included a monumental staircase leading to the main entrance and abundant additions of sculpture.

As luxurious as the facade, the great interior hall has an airy, lighter feel. Its crowning feature is an elliptical rotunda that lifts the eye upward to a magnificent skylight floating above the space without visible signs of support. In 1937, the acclaimed artist Reginald Marsh (1898–1954) accepted a low-paying position with the Treasury Department to paint murals encircling the rotunda dome. Although trade and commerce had slowed considerably by this point in the Depression, Marsh's vivid paintings, a mixture of con-

temporary and historic scenes, expressed the city's status as a great port and also celebrated Columbus and other explorers of the American continent.

However, as shipping through the port of New York continued to decline in the years ahead, the Custom House eventually took on a different purpose and theme. In the 1950s and 1960s, New York City docks lost ground to New Jersey containerports, the innovative, larger facilities that required much more room than Manhattan could provide. One by one, the major shipping companies defected to New Jersey and the old piers that lined Manhattan's waterfront shut down. In 1973, U.S. Customs, unable to maintain the lavish building, moved to modern quarters in the new World Trade Center just completed a few blocks to the north by the Port Authority of New York and New Jersey.

The Custom House eventually took in new tenants, both quite different from the original occupants. The upper floors now house the U.S. Bankruptcy Court, an ironic change in the building's preoccupation from wealth to debt. The main floor, the domain of the National Museum of the American Indian, includes the vast collection of George Gustav Heye, a New Yorker who assembled a million Indian artifacts from North, Central, and South America in the first half of the twentieth century. The museum acts as a modern antidote to the past portrayal of subjugated native people as the price of American progress.

Left: The crowning feature of the interior is an elliptical rotunda topped by a skylight that seems to float above the splendid room. Vivid murals painted by Reginald Marsh in 1937 encircle the dome and celebrate the city's leading role in trade and commerce.

Right: The richly decorated vaulted ceilings reflect the prosperity of the nation in the early twentieth century.

Flatiron Building

Architect: Daniel Burnham

Built: 1901–1903

Often mistaken for New York City's first skyscraper, the Flatiron Building was the first tall building to soar north of City Hall and launched the city's skyscraper era that took off at the turn of the twentieth century. Dozens of earlier buildings had been built with the same inner strength, a steel skeleton, that allowed buildings to rise to new heights in the late nineteenth century. And many taller buildings would follow in the intense period of construction of the early 1900s.

But even without a title to its name, the Flatiron became a skyscraper icon, an unmistakable symbol of the city throughout the next century. Rising on a triangular island between Fifth Avenue and Broadway, it literally stands out on its own.

Ironically, this image of New York City is the work of an architect almost solely identified with Chicago. Daniel Burnham is best known for designing a grand plan for Chicago in 1909 and for his motto, "Make no small plans." He came to New York after rising to national prominence as the head of the 1893 World Columbian Exposition in Chicago where he ensconced Neo-Classicism as America's building style for much of the twentieth century. Yet he made the Flatiron Building a singular piece of work.

Although the building is clad in Italian Renaissance dress, its figure is a modern slab.

Far Right: Rising like the prow of a great ship, the Flatiron has been a romantic icon of New York City for an entire century.

Right: The ornate façade belies the Flatiron's steel skeleton.

Built out to the lot line on all sides of its triangular site, it soars upward and appears much taller than its twenty-three stories. The apex of the triangle is only six feet wide and from the side, the building looks like a single thick wall. Head on, it can look like an approaching locomotive, and the metal and glass extension at the base of the apex is appropriately called "the cowcatcher." A later addition, it hides two grand columns that once marked the point of the triangle.

Originally called the Fuller Building, it was soon known by its flatiron shape and the name was changed accordingly. But a closer look at the sidewalls reveals that the building is not actually flat. The brick and terra-cotta façade undulates over bay windows that project out from both sides of the wedge. The ripple effect can make the building shimmer, as though its walls were the sails of a giant ship making its way up the avenue. The illusion of movement is all the more apparent on

the building's windy, freestanding site. At the time of its completion, the public, still wary of skyscrapers, feared the tower would topple and called it "Burnham's Folly."

The slab did create downdrafts, but with a much gentler result of lifting women's skirts. Legend has it that a popular phrase of the day, "Twenty-three skidoo," came from policemen shooing away men gawking at wind-blown women passing by on Twenty-third Street.

Left: Even when seen on its own, the narrow apex of the triangular roofline is unmistakable as the Flatiron Building.

Right: A detail of the building's terra-cotta façade.

The Flatiron was completed in 1903 and before the end of the decade, two buildings would rise at more than double its height: the Singer Building in Lower Manhattan at forty-seven stories and the Metropolitan Life Building on Madison Square at fifty. While different in size, all three buildings were driven by the same commercial force that pushed skyscrapers to take up most of their sites. Yet the Flatiron's artful form was perceived as much more than just a business venture. Edward Steichen and Alfred Steiglitz photographed it as a mystical tower rising out of the haze. The images, among the most famous of these now-famous photographers, captured the public's imagination, then and now. Unencumbered by changes around it, the century-old building is still an island unto itself and one of New York City's most romantic symbols.

Grand Central Terminal

Architects: Reed & Stem and Warren & Wetmore; engineer, William Wilgus

Built: 1903–1913

The story of Grand Central Terminal is more than the tale of a single building. It is the saga of how a railroad empire created, nearly destroyed, and finally restored what critics believe is America's greatest work of architecture and engineering. The terminal opened in 1913 as the crowning glory of Cornelius Vanderbilt's New York Central Railroad. In the second half of the twentieth century, it became a liability to Vanderbilt's financially strapped successors, and the cause célèbre of the city's most successful historic preservation campaign. The controversy focused on the main terminal, a majestic Beaux-Arts building housing a monumental concourse, but this was only part of the building's achievement.

Grand Central was the second railroad terminal at 42nd Street. The first, built in 1871, was then at the outskirts of the city and critics complained that it was "neither grand nor central." But the railroad had little choice in picking

Far Right: Built in the glory days of railroad travel, the terminal's majestic building had to fight for its life from the 1950s through the 1970s, a battle finally settled in the U.S. Supreme Court. The Met Life Tower behind it was called a "monstrous bland blanket" when it cut off sweeping views of Park Avenue in 1963. Elevated on a platform, the triumphal terminal still enjoys a commanding presence in the heart of Midtown.

Right: Even the passageways in the terminal have striking features such as this skylight and glorious chandelier.

the location. Noisy and dirty, steam-powered trains were banned south of 42nd Street. North of the terminal, the area was a chaotic, dangerous expanse of open tracks. In 1902, after a collision of two trains in a steam-filled tunnel killed seventeen passengers, the city required all tracks to be electrified. For the New York Central, this meant refurbishing thirty-seven station tracks between 42nd Street and the northern reaches of the city. In a daring plan, William Wilgus, the chief engineer, proposed sweeping away the old system and building a gigantic complex centered at 42nd Street. His plan included seventy tracks running underground on two levels and supported by a "submerged forest of columns." This intricate system and the magnificent new terminal building were constructed over the better part of a decade while the old terminal continued operating.

Wilgus' genius went beyond railroad engineering to envision a new urban fabric. The new terminal building at 42nd Street covers less than ten percent of the underground track system. The rest extends east, west, and north of the building beneath a dozen blocks. Once the tracks were built, the area was covered to create new streets. Free of smoke, noise, and soot, much of the area became the elegant Park Avenue that New Yorkers know today. Wilgus also came up with a brilliant way to pay for the project and capture new revenue. The railroad sold the "air rights" above the tracks to private developers who built office buildings, hotels, and other new facilities, many connected underground to the terminal.

The team of architects working on the main terminal made it a superb embodiment of the project's monumental character. Elevated on a platform with a triumphal triple-arched façade, the building became a grand gateway to New York City. Inside, great arched windows and a vaulted ceiling traced with starlit constellations made the concourse the premier public space in the nation. But by the 1950s, with highways outpacing train service, the railroad was looking for

Left: Critics consider the terminal's main concourse "the finest big room in the nation." The awesome space was once threatened with radical alterations and demolition, but after a successful campaign to preserve it, it was finally restored in 1998.

Right: The terminal's crowning sculpture, Mercury astride an eagle, is one of the features that is as well known as the building itself.

more income and introduced commercial intrusions into the grand space. A giant screen advertising Kodak film stretched across one wall of windows, blocking the glorious shafts of light that had streamed into the great room. The ceiling lights of the zodiac went out and grime further darkened the concourse and stained the granite and limestone façade.

In 1954, the railroad announced plans to demolish the neglected building and in the following decade entertained every conceivable plan designed to profit by what had become a prime commercial location. But these schemes met with great resistance from the press and public. When Penn Station was destroyed, this led to the city's first historic preservation law in 1965 and to landmark protection for Grand Central's façade in 1967. Undaunted, New York Central and a private developer hired Marcel Breuer to design a fifty-five-story slab above the Beaux-Arts façade. Fearing a radically altered terminal, Jacquelyn Kennedy Onassis led a preservation campaign that gathered citywide support. The city's Landmark Preservation Commission turned down the skyscraper scheme, but the railroad challenged the decision. After years of lawsuits, the case reached the U.S. Supreme Court, the first historic preservation battle to get that far, and in 1978, the court upheld the landmark protection.

In 1998, architects Beyer, Blinder, Belle completely restored the concourse. The Kodak screen came down and a marble staircase went up in its place, a new match for the grand steps that once graced only the opposite side of the room. The cerulean blue ceiling was cleaned and the stars were lit once again, restoring its unusual perspective. Seen from below, the constellations are reversed, allowing the public to see them "as God would from the heavens above." Filled with bustling shops and restaurants, the concourse is a vibrant place for social interaction and a source of urban inspiration to the tens of thousands who pass through everyday.

Woolworth Building

Architect: Cass Gilbert

Built: 1910–1913

The tallest building in the world for the first seventeen years of its life, the Woolworth Building reigned over the New York City skyline until it lost its title to the Chrysler Building in 1930. But like all great skyscrapers, the Woolworth's height, some sixty stories, nearly 800 feet, was not the only reason for its lasting fame. Widely acclaimed when it was completed in 1913, it was disdained for its ornate neo-Gothic façade in the 1950s by modernist architects who maintained that skyscrapers ought to be a pure expression of height and structural engineering. After decades of spare, modern buildings, the Woolworth is greatly appreciated once again. Paul Goldberger, the former architecture critic for the *New York Times*, ranks it among the greatest skyscrapers ever created.

The first skyscrapers appeared in the late nineteenth century as the evolution of advances in steam-powered elevators and steel construction. But even by the twentieth century, builders and

Right: Rising over City Hall Park, the Woolworth tower soars up from its wide base like the long neck of a majestic steed.

Left: The Gothic details of the façade made the Woolworth famous as "the Cathedral of Commerce."

architects were not ready to relinquish the styles of the past to the technology of the future. The Woolworth captured the best of both worlds.

Its builder, F. W. Woolworth, the founder of the five-and-dime stores, had one overreaching goal—to make his building the tallest in the world. Surprisingly, he chose an architect with little experience in skyscrapers, Cass Gilbert, who was grounded in the Beaux-Arts tradition of ordered, classical design. For his new commission, Gilbert chose another historic style, neo-Gothic. While it recalled medieval churches, the tallest buildings of that age, in Gilbert's hands, the soaring, pointed arches of the Gothic style seemed made for modern skyscrapers.

The Woolworth's size, shape, and ornament are perfectly matched. The building rests on a massive base that fills an entire block facing City Hall Park. The tower rises from the park side of the base like the long neck of a majestic steed and continues the building's vertical lines without visual interruption. Despite its considerable mass, the structure soars up to a pinnacled crown and the thin, white lines of the terra-cotta façade reinforce the vertical ascent. Gothic detail also abounds inside the vaulted lobby where mosaic ceiling tiles, gilded ironwork, and terrazzo floors

Right: Like a Byzantine church, the vaulted lobby ceilings are richly inlaid with mosaic tiles.

create an exotic atmosphere redolent of Byzantine churches.

To Gilbert, the Gothic style gave the building "the greatest degree of aspiration...and spirituality," words echoed by the Rev. S. Parkes Cadman, a leading clergyman of the day, who dubbed the building the "Cathedral of Commerce." Although the title may sound ironic to modern ears, American architects and clergymen in the early twentieth century were perfectly comfortable with ascribing spiritual qualities to a commercial building and comparing the benefits of religion and commerce. In a brochure about the building, Cadman wrote, "Just as religion monopolized art and architecture during the Medieval epoch, so commerce has engrossed the United States since 1865...Out of the struggle...have been developed gratifying benefits...Here on the Island of Manhattan...the Woolworth is acknowledged as premier..."

The Woolworth Building was also unique in the annals of commercial development. Frank Woolworth paid more than thirteen million dollars—in cash—to construct the building and his company retained ownership for the next eighty-five years before finally selling it in 1998 for 155 million dollars. Once an institution in small-town America, Woolworth stores have disappeared, but the Woolworth Building remains an architectural legend in New York. Its builders are remembered not only for their achievement, but also for their sense of humor. The serious Gothic interior has playful gargoyles, caricatures of the major figures responsible for the building, its engineer, rental agent, banker, and even the architect and owner. In the corners of the lobby, Gilbert cradles a model of the building and Woolworth counts his nickels and dimes.

Riverside Church

Architects: Allen & Collens and Henry Pelton

Built: 1926–1930

Rising twenty-four stories above the Hudson River and built on a steel frame, this is New York City's quintessential skyscraper church. While other churches began to look more like commercial towers in the first decades of the twentieth century, Riverside reached the pinnacle of ecclesiastical grandiosity.

Competing for a place in the New York skyline, skyscrapers and churches swapped architectural styles and building techniques. In church-like Gothic garb, the Woolworth Building soared into the heavens in 1913, dwarfing the nineteenth-century steeples of Trinity Church and St. Paul's Chapel. The Convocation Tower, a colossal church proposed for Madison Square in 1921, aspired to 1000 feet, yet never began construction. As commercial buildings marched up the island, churches felt the squeeze of rising land costs. Some congregations, following Grand Central Terminal's lead, built new church buildings by selling off part of their valuable property for commercial development. But for Riverside Church, money was no object. The congregation was blessed with one of the nation's wealthiest men as its leading member and prime benefactor, John D. Rockefeller Jr.

In 1926, Rockefeller convinced his parish, the Park Avenue Baptist Church, to leave the building it had completed just four years earlier

Right: The ultimate skyscraper church, Riverside rises nearly 400 feet, with the world's largest carillon at the top and basketball courts and a bowling alley below.

Far Right: Loosely based on Chartres Cathedral, the church tower brought the French Gothic style to Harlem.

at 64th Street for a more imposing and spacious setting uptown. St. John the Divine had led the way in the 1890s by breaking ground for a cathedral at 110th Street, but by the 1920s even that huge project was surrounded by development and no longer stood out from a distance. Rockefeller had a better site in mind, a high point of land overlooking the Hudson in the fashionable Morningside Heights neighborhood where Columbia University had founded a stately home in the late nineteenth century.

The move was also inspired by religious changes. Like many churches of the time, the Park Avenue Baptist Church had assumed broader social and educational responsibilities and needed space for classrooms, meeting rooms, and other facilities. But Rockefeller's most compelling reason to move was his adherence to religious reform and to the principles of the congregation's

controversial pastor, Henry Emerson Fosdick. A theological liberal, Fosdick wanted to open the congregation to all Christian sects, serving the city's diverse mix of races and nationalities. It was Fosdick's idea to move uptown, near Columbia's intellectual center and the neighborhood's diverse mix of residents.

Although the leaders of this liberal congregation were casting off old practices, like total baptismal immersion, they wanted their new church to have a cloak of historic architectural tradition. They selected the same architects, Allen & Collens and Henry Pelton, who had designed their Gothic Park Avenue building. The design of the new church was also Gothic, replete with arches, pinnacles, buttresses, and stained glass,

Left: Intricate carvings and sculpture adorn the exterior.

Right: Magnificent ribbed arches lead to the main sanctuary.

but the scale was immense, incorporating facilities never imagined by medieval architects. Loosely based on Chartres Cathedral in France, the Laura Spelman Rockefeller Memorial Tower rose nearly 400 feet high, housing church offices, social facilities, and the world's largest carillon—all accessible by the highest elevator shafts ever installed in a church. The huge auditorium was capable of seating 2,400 worshippers with ample room below for a bowling alley, basketball court, and theater.

Some critics of the day complained that Riverside's style was overdone, calling it "scrambled Gothic." At the same time, they hailed the great nave as a place of "real beauty and fine proportions." Funded primarily by Rockefeller, the church was built with the finest materials available and has stone carvings and stained glass of timeless craftsmanship, including Flemish windows from a sixteenth-century church.

Over its seventy-year life, Riverside has maintained its liberal tradition and serves a nonsectarian, interracial congregation largely drawn from nearby Harlem and Columbia University. A prominent citywide forum, it has attracted internationally known figures, including the Rev. Martin Luther King Jr. who delivered his famous anti-Vietnam War sermon from the pulpit, and Nelson Mandela who spoke at an interfaith celebration on his first visit to America. While tall buildings continued to march uptown, the church still stands tall above the Hudson, the most distinctive structure on the riverfront from Midtown to the George Washington Bridge.

Chrysler Building

Architect: William Van Alen

Built: 1928–1930

Like no other skyscraper had done before, the Chrysler Building brought a vision of fantasy to the New York skyline. Its pointed silver dome, a rocket ship from a Hollywood version of space travel, seemed to come from another world. The illusion still captures the imagination. Seventy-seven stories high, the Chrysler Building was the winner of a frenzied race to build the world's tallest building, only to lose the title less than a year later to the 102-story Empire State Building. But the Chrysler Building always stood for much more than height. Fabulously modern in 1930, it was the gleaming embodiment of architecture's jazz age and the epitome of corporate splendor.

Surprisingly, the Chrysler Corporation did not initiate the project. It started with William Reynolds who had developed Dreamland, a fantasy-world amusement park in Coney Island in 1904. Reynolds hired the architect for the skyscraper, William Van Alen, a talented maverick who had captured the Paris Prize at the Beaux Arts Institute of Design in 1908, but later swore off Old World traditions. Beset by financial problems, Reynolds soon sold his interest in the project to automobile magnate Walter Chrysler. Unlike most skyscraper developers in this competitive age, Chrysler cared more

Far Right: The Chrysler Building rises from a massive base to an amazing lightness and grace in the dome and slender spire.

Right: Every detail, like this Art Deco glass at the entrance, was expressed with stylized perfection.

about design than height, but Van Alen persuaded him that both were essential to the building's success.

Chrysler and Van Alen worked in close collaboration. Although the building is called Art Deco, a motif promoted by the stylized designs of a 1925 Parisian exhibition, it is clearly a unique creation, the result of two inventive minds. Two brick wings flanking the main entrance reach out to Lexington Avenue like the arms of the Sphinx. From this massive base, the tower rises to an amazing lightness and grace in the dome and slender spire.

Moving forward with amazing speed, the building construction entered a fever-pitched race for the sky in the final months of the roaring twenties. The Chrysler Building was neck and neck with several other Manhattan skyscrapers competing to become the world's tallest tower. One in particular spurred Van Alen's intense desire to win. The Bank of Manhattan Building at 40 Wall Street was the work of Van Alen's former partner, H. Craig Severance. The competition became a personal battle as the architects, taking their cue from each other's plans, kept increasing the number of floors. Van Alen finally devised a secret plan, a 185-foot-high spire that he hid inside an airshaft. Once Severance topped off his building at seventy-one floors, Van Alen gave the signal to raise the twenty-seven-ton spire to its crowning glory, surpassing his rival by 121 feet.

Although the Chrysler Building won the race, critics were less than enthusiastic about the design. The stock market crash in 1929 and the completion of the Empire State Building in 1931 also eclipsed the Chrysler's achievement. The Depression ended the skyscraper boom and halted Van Alen's career. After a dispute with Chrysler, he never designed another major building. Yet, during these hard times, the Chrysler Building was a financial success. While the new champion of the skyline became known as the "Empty State Building," the Chrysler had a full roster of corporate tenants, including the Texaco Oil Company, which occupied more than a quarter of the building. A brotherhood of oil, steel, and automobile executives enjoyed each other's company in the lavish Cloud Club on three linked floors just below the dome. The public paid fifty cents each to enter the 71st floor observatory, the interior of the pointed dome, which offered views from the triangular windows. Lit by Saturn-like milky glass and steel fixtures, the atmospheric space looked like a set for *The Cabinet of Doctor Caligari*, a German Expressionist film of the 1920s.

However, while the Empire State Building survived on revenue from its popular observation deck, the Chrysler observatory was a financial disappointment and closed in 1945. The postwar years brought continued competition from other office buildings, peaking in a surge of new buildings, including the World Trade Center in Lower Manhattan, that glutted the market in the 1970s. At the bottom of New York City's economic slide in 1975, Texaco left for the suburbs and the Chrysler Building was virtually empty. With cracked walls, broken elevators, and leaks in the dome, the building went into foreclosure and was sold for 35 million dollars. Fortunately, the new owner did not forsake the building's proud past, but instead invested nearly as much as the purchase price in repairs and renovations. Two decades later, the Chrysler was sold again, this time for 220 million dollars. A total restoration completed in 2002 has brought the building back to its shining, showy self.

Once criticized as ostentatious, the Chrysler Building is popular today—precisely for its flashy style. Its gigantic automotive flourishes are still more impressive than any make of car. Its theatrical lobby continues to pull people in from the street just to admire the stylized design. Its famous

Cloud Club and observation deck, like the movies that inspired their design, now exist only in pictures, but they still have legions of devoted fans.

Left: Gigantic eagles project from all sides of the 61st Street story. A world apart from their Gothic predecessors, these gargoyles could be hood ornaments for gigantic cars. A line of Chrysler hubcaps also speeds along the intricate striped façade toward enormous radiator caps at the building's corners. The wonderful details are hand-fabricated steel, made by a man who later became a special effects artist in Hollywood where he created Xanadu, the fantastic estate in *Citizen Kane*.

Empire State Building

Architects: Shreve, Lamb, and Harmon

Built: 1929–1931

The Empire State Building is a monolith with style. Handsome and well proportioned, the powerful structure is smartly dressed in gray stone with black granite and steel trim. Wearing the same conservative uniform all its life, the sharp-edged tower has been a serious, square-jawed sentinel watching over the city for more than seventy years. Reaching 102 stories in 1931, it was the tallest in the world for nearly half a century until the completion of the 110-story World Trade Center towers in the 1970s. Since September 11, the Empire State has domi-nated the skyline once again, a solemn king of the sky.

Right: The tower is a mighty, uninterrupted shaft that accommodates 6,500 windows. Built in an age without air-conditioning, it promised every office worker light and fresh air.

Left: Entering the lobby, three stories high and 100 feet long, one immediately looks toward the back wall where an aluminum outline of the building is inlaid on black marble. Superimposed on a map of New York, the image makes it clear that both New York and the building are the Empire State.

Left: Long windows, nearly five stories high, rise above the commanding Fifth Avenue entrance.

Right: Bronze medallions on the marble lobby walls honor the industries and trades that produced the building in record time. This one is highlighted by the reflection of a flag hanging above.

The Empire State is a child of the Depression, it has weathered hard times and earned its place as the iconic namesake of New York State. When the stock market crashed in 1929, the Empire State was still in its early planning stages, yet the project was rushed head-on into construction. Driven by the former financial chief of General Motors who wanted to surpass the height of the Chrysler Building, the Empire State investors had high hopes for success. With so many skyscrapers on the drawing boards in the 1920s, large Manhattan building sites in good locations were rare. The Empire State had a choice spot, the former home of the Waldorf-Astoria Hotel. A jewel of New York's Gilded Age and the center of society at the turn of the nineteenth century, the hotel died of thirst during Prohibition and was demolished in 1928. The fashionable set had passed it by, but its prominent site at the corner of Fifth Avenue and 34th Street had a promising future as an office center.

The architects, Shreve, Lamb, and Harmon, were given a tight budget and a tall order. They developed an impressive yet practical building plan, concentrating as many offices as possible within the tower where the occupants could enjoy unobstructed light and air. These features were major selling points at a time when tall buildings were standing shoulder to shoulder in Wall Street—without the benefit of air conditioning. The spokesman for the project, former New York State Governor Al Smith, proclaimed that the Empire State, the only skyscraper to come even close to 100 stories, could go up "without endangering the health of tenants or neighbors." Rising from a five-story base, the rest of the building was a mighty, uninterrupted shaft that

accommodated 6,500 windows. No office would be without one.

All towering hulk, the Empire State is a contradiction in terms, yet it works nonetheless. The building's details give it soaring power and grace. The windows are handsomely highlighted in long, unbroken lines of steel and aluminum trim, accentuating the tower's vertical ascent. Even the base rises monumentally with colossal pilasters flanking its commanding Fifth Avenue entrance.

The pace of construction set a new record, reaching completion in fifteen months—just in time to greet the start of the Depression. Known as the "Empty State" for nearly a decade, the building was saved from financial ruin by the attraction of its crowning feature, a winged spire of steel, aluminum, nickel, and glass. The architects had designed a flat top for the building, but the owners insisted on the spire as a "mooring mast" for dirigibles. Used only twice, the mast was derided by architecture critic Lewis Mumford as "a public comfort station for migratory birds." Once the space below the spire was converted to an observation deck, thousands of paying customers flocked to the top of the building, which brought in a constant stream of revenue.

The spire became even more popular after a giant gorilla climbed it in the 1933 movie, *King Kong*. (The film premiered at Radio City Music Hall in Rockefeller Center and also gave that new development a boost.) Ironically, when *King Kong* was remade in 1976, a giant balloon of the gorilla that was attached to the mast as a promotion failed to stay up. Yet, once again, the public's fascination with the spire never waned. Even when the twin towers dominated the skyline, the Empire State's illuminated crown continued to charm the public, celebrating the holidays with changing colored lights, green for St. Patrick's Day, yellow and orange for Halloween, and red and green for Christmas. After the trade towers fell, the Empire State lights were red, white, and blue for nearly a year. Back to their regular schedule, they are a signal to the city that even after great tragedy, life goes on. The building crown is once again New York City's beacon, a constant presence in the skyline, as familiar and comforting as an old friend.

Rockefeller Center

Architects: Reinhard & Hofmeister; Corbett, Harrison & MacMurray;

Raymond Hood, Godley & Fouilhoux

Built: 1932–1940

New York skyscrapers had always been an independent breed, each one asserting its own personality and rearing up above the herd. Rockefeller Center was the first time architects corralled a group of towers into an organized plan. Criticized at first for its enormous size, the center was later seen as ahead of its time and the premier urban complex of the twentieth century.

Covering several blocks in the heart of Midtown, the complex is a coordinated collection of office towers, theaters, and restaurants, all connected to a public plaza and underground shopping concourse. To a 1930s New York City, the size of the project was mind boggling. The office towers covered as much ground as thirteen Chrysler Building sites and provided as much office space as two Empire State Buildings. Built during the worst years of the Depression, the vast complex was the largest private real estate venture ever undertaken in the city.

WISDOM AND KNOWLEDGE SHALL BE THE STABILITY OF THY TIMES

Right: Rising in the center of the complex is a slender seventy-story tower, originally called the RCA Building and now known as the GE Building. Like the buildings gathered around it, the tower is tailored in form-fitting limestone and faces Rockefeller Plaza, a lively public space in the middle of the project. This view is looking west from Fifth Avenue. The space between the two foreground buildings is the Channel Gardens, named for the English Channel because it passes between buildings occupied by English and French shops.

Left: All of the buildings in the complex are embellished with artwork focusing on monumental themes. The art enhanced the architecture and, at the same time, offset some of the early criticism of this massive commercial development.

Left: Patrons of modern art, the Rockefellers commissioned many contemporary artists to contribute works to the development, such as this stainless steel piece on the Associated Press Building by sculptor Isamu Noguchi. The family also founded the Museum of Modern Art, a few blocks north of the complex.

The project was advanced by two of the most powerful businessmen in the country, John D. Rockefeller Jr., who had inherited his father's Standard Oil fortune, and Owen Young, the Chairman of General Electric. Conceived as a grand home for a new Metropolitan Opera House, it evolved into Radio City, a center for GE's radio networks, RCA and NBC, and later for their television studios. It gave popular culture a place of honor in the city and also marked the debut of a young man who would become a political powerhouse, Rockefeller's son, Nelson, New York State Governor from 1958 to 1973 and United States Vice President in 1974.

After the opera pulled out of the project, John D. Rockefeller, who had assembled the property for the development, gave GE the starring role. In place of the opera house, the central feature became the seventy-story RCA Building. Molded by Raymond Hood, the renowned architect of New York's Daily News and McGraw Hill Buildings and Chicago's Tribune Tower, the skyscraper had a radically new form. It rose not from a base, but directly from the street into a slender slab with thin wings that seemed to float along its sides.

Despite many other innovative features created by the team of eight leading architects, critics were wary of the impact the huge commercial project would have on the city, particularly without the sanctifying presence of the opera. The developers responded with a cultural counter-offensive. In a barrage of press releases, they announced that the buildings would have embellishments worthy of a great development, based on a theme of "Man the Builder." However, their first grand gesture backfired. Hood and others made an expedition to Europe to invite the greatest artists of the day, Picasso, Matisse, and others, to submit ideas for the RCA lobby murals, but only Diego Rivera was willing to take the commission.

Nelson Rockefeller had suggested Rivera, overcoming his father's skepticism about the painter's affiliation with the Communist Party. Unfortunately for the twenty-four-year-old Nelson, his father's worst fears proved true. Rivera painted the lobby walls with powerful scenes of labor demonstrations, highlighted in dominant shades of red. He placed the final straw on the camel's back when he put Lenin's likeness on one of the figures and ignored Nelson's demand to remove the portrait. The press had a field day with "a capitalist footing the bill for Communist activity." Rivera was fired and the murals were destroyed, replaced by apolitical artwork.

To many New Yorkers, Rockefeller Center is not a group of buildings but rather its celebrated public plaza. The sunken space is the centerpiece of the complex and is highly visible from terraces and walkways on all sides. It is filled with year-round activity—café tables in spring and summer and in winter a popular skating rink and huge Christmas tree nearly as tall as a skyscraper. One of the first public spaces in an office district, it drew people to the center of the city on weekends as well as workdays and created a new sense of urban vitality.

Struggling during its early years, Radio City got out of the red and, to the amazement of the city's declining real estate community, started to expand in 1934. The International Building continued the handsome frontage of new buildings along Fifth Avenue. Within a few years, the Associated Press, U.S. Rubber Company, and other buildings were also up and occupied. With considerable connections to many different industries, the oil-rich Rockefellers always seemed to be able to rent their buildings, even if many of the tenants were their own companies. Before the

end of the 1930s, as one historian observed, "the Rockefellers put their name where their money was" and Radio City became Rockefeller Center. Although the family has sold a substantial part of the complex, which has grown to nineteen commercial buildings, it still bears the family name. Just as Nelson Rockefeller proclaimed in 1939, Rockefeller Center is more than a development, it is "a Civic Institution."

Left: Rockefeller Center included the largest theater of its time, Radio City Music Hall. Opened at the start of the Depression, the theater lost tens of thousands of dollars in its first weeks of operation, ending the career of its legendary impresario, Samuel Roxy. Today, it is one of the city's most popular venues.

United Nations Headquarters

Architects: International Committee. Wallace K. Harrison—Chairman

Built: 1947–1953

After World War II, as London, Paris, Berlin, and Tokyo lay damaged, demoralized, or in ruins, New York emerged as the world's leading city. No single building better represented this fact than the United Nations Secretariat. Standing unobstructed along Manhattan's East River water-front, the tower established New York as the international capital of the world. Its striking form, a narrow slab bare of decoration, ushered in a new age of architectural modernism. The most prominent building in the United Nations complex, the Secretariat tower was New York City's first glass curtain wall, a type of construction that changed the face of modern architecture. Developed in Europe in the 1920s, the modernist style was still a radical choice for a government building in the 1940s. Devoid of all historic details, it signaled a determination to forego the past and face the future.

Creating the New York site for the United Nations was as visionary as the project itself. For more than a century, this stretch of First Avenue, now called United Nations Plaza, had been known as Blood Alley, complete with slaughter houses, cattle pens, and a stench that turned stomachs across Midtown. In 1946, real estate mogul

Right: The Secretariat Building's striking glass form ushered in a new age of architectural modernism.

Far Right: The Dag Hammarskjold Library, foreground, is one of three long, low buildings grouped at the base of the Secretariat tower. The library was added in 1961 to honor the UN's late Secretary General.

William Zeckendorf entered into an agreement to purchase the land from the meat packing companies. Inspired by Grand Central Terminal's development of Park Avenue, he envisioned a "city within the city," a massive expanse of modern buildings rising on a riverfront platform. At the same time, New York City was in a tight race with Philadelphia to become the home of the United Nations, but Robert Moses, New York's master builder, a man who usually got his way, was promoting a site in Queens.

Just as the United Nations was about to approve Philadelphia, Zeckendorf offered to sell the First Avenue land to New York City. Mayor William O'Dwyer called in a key member of his UN committee, Nelson Rockefeller, and within days, his father, John D. Rockefeller Jr., purchased the land for eight and a half million dollars and donated it to the city. A week after Zeckendorf made his offer, the UN approved the Manhattan site as its future home.

The lead architect for the United Nations, Wallace K. Harrison, was perfectly positioned for the job, having worked for the Rockefellers, Zeckendorf, and Moses. Harrison assembled an international team of architects representing the UN's principal nations. The notable exceptions, Ludwig Mies van der Rohe and Marcel Breuer, were left out because their German background was politically unpalatable so soon after the war. Although French architect Le Corbusier contributed the basic concept for the project, his cantankerous personality led to his exclusion from the construction process.

Yet the design reflected the thinking of these modernist masters who first called for buildings stripped to their bare essentials in the 1920s. Mies had proposed glass curtain wall buildings at that time, but it would take the technology of postwar America to realize his vision. Curtain walls went hand in hand with steel frame construction. Instead of thick masonry walls holding up the building, the steel skeleton bore the weight and the walls could be hung on the frame like a curtain. While early skyscrapers had steel frames, they were usually covered by decorative brick, marble, or limestone. The modernists favored glass because it expressed the building's inherent structure. But it would take years to perfect glass panes that were both thin and strong enough to serve as window walls, and to devise foolproof methods of hanging the glass on the frame.

The Secretariat achieved this goal with great art. The 544-foot-high tower is a pure rectangle, 287 feet wide and only 72 feet thick. The narrow ends are marble, emphasizing the expanse of glass on both sides. The panes are attached to an aluminum grid that projects nearly three feet beyond the steel skeleton, creating the illusion of uninterrupted glass. Since these wide walls face east and west, they were covered with an innovative heat-absorbing glass, tinted blue-green. The tower is set off by long, low buildings, of which the most prominent is the General Assembly. Deceptively simple, its sweeping concave roof and dome are as distinctive as the Secretariat. While the General Assembly is a familiar space, thanks to televised coverage of its meetings, the Secretariat is the private domain of UN staff. Arriving at the end of the Depression and the war, the UN ended more than a decade of decline in New York City's construction industry and was the start of an office building boom that lasted through the end of the century.

The UN still enjoys a prominent place on the waterfront, but unfortunately, while new buildings sprouted up around it, the Secretariat, besieged by international concerns and budget problems, requires a total renovation. UN officials are planning to build another tower to house staff during the renovation on the site of the Robert Moses Playground, named for the man who wanted the UN to be built in Queens. The late builder is no longer here to protest and his wishes will be overruled once again when the playground is razed to make way for another Manhattan tower.

Above Left: The narrow marble ends of the Secretariat tower emphasize its wide glass walls.

Right: The vertical Secretariat tower and the horizontal General Assembly Building, right, create a dramatic contrast.

Lever House

Architect: Gordon Bunshaft of Skidmore, Owings & Merrill

Built: 1950–1952

Compared to any number of modern office towers that followed it, the Lever House stands out like a glass jewel. Its unique qualities are also apparent in a less obvious comparison with a jewel of a much earlier era—the Flatiron Building. Distant cousins of the skyscraper clan, the 1903 Flatiron and the 1952 Lever House are about the same height. Dissimilar in every other feature, their differences are more than skin deep.

The Flatiron's brick and terra-cotta façade and the Lever House's glass exterior are mere reflections of the different technologies of their age. Their completely different building forms are worlds apart in architectural and corporate thinking. Like most skyscrapers before and after it, the Flatiron used every possible square foot of its site for commercial return. Half a century later, the Lever Corporation, a thoroughly commercial enterprise, chose aesthetics over profits to create a building covering only a quarter of its available site.

A unique departure from the bigger-is-better trend, the twenty-one-story Lever House was well below the size permitted by city zoning. From the start, the corporation decided to limit the office space to the amount needed for staff. A larger building would have brought in additional revenue, but it also would have been subject to zoning regulations that might have led to a typical design. Enacted in 1916 (well after the Flatiron was built), the regulations required buildings that

Left: Placed at right angles to the street, Lever House "floats" above Park Avenue like a "waterfall frozen in mid-tumble."

Right: Enclosed in clear glass, the entrance reflects a line of corporate towers built after Lever House.

covered their lot to rise like a wedding cake in a series of tiers designed to allow sufficient light and air. Covering only a fraction of its site, Lever House broke the mold to become the city's first skyscraper rendered in pure geometric forms.

The building is comprised of two simple slabs, a horizontal base, only one story high, and a slender vertical tower. The architect emphasized the separate box-like forms by setting each one on columns. The two boxes housed different functions, mail and stock rooms below and offices in the tower above. Physically connected, they come together brilliantly as an aesthetic whole. Like the much taller United Nations Secretariat Building, the Lever House was inspired by the European masters of modern architecture who favored glass as a sheer reflection of functional design. But without the Secretariat's marble-covered ends, it is a more perfect example of a glass box. Even the spandrels, the space between the windows, are glass, creating a continuous wall. Enveloped in blue-green glass, the Lever House, according to author Wayne Curtis, is "a waterfall frozen in mid tumble."

This new symbol of corporate modernity included considerable benefits for employees. The base was cut out to allow light on a court-yard below and the rest of the roof was landscaped as a garden. From inside the offices, the small slim tower, only fifty-three feet wide, is all windows, light, and views. Since the windows do not open, the architects devised the first automated window washing system that moves around the building on cables suspended from the roof. For the Lever Corporation, which manufactured soap, the

Left: Lever House is composed of pure geometric forms.

Below Left: The base and tower are each elevated on columns, emphasizing the separate components of the building.

Right: A perfect glass box, the building was completely restored with new glass in 2002.

system was a built-in advertisement. The gleaming glass building was a dramatic contrast to its masonry neighbors on Park Avenue. In an even more radical move, the tower was placed at right angles to the avenue, breaking out of the uniformity of the street wall. The perpendicular placement made the aquamarine tower "float" above the street in pristine isolation from its neighbors. Like all bold designs, it elicited strong reactions.

A decade after it was built, Yale's celebrated architectural historian Vincent Scully said the placement of the tower "cut a hole in the wall that defined the avenue." Scully's real complaint was with the anonymous glass boxes that followed Lever House, diminishing the building's unique presence and the integrity of Park Avenue. Although more of these boxes would follow in the decades to come, the Lever House, totally restored in recent years, still stands out from its lesser imitations. Like Cinderella, it is the only one that truly fits its glass slipper.

Seagram Building

Architects: Ludwig Mies van der Rohe with Philip Johnson and Kahn & Jacobs

Built: 1955–1958

Ludwig Mies van der Rohe designed only one building in New York City, but when he got the chance to create a Manhattan office tower, this master of modernity left some of his earlier austerity behind and created a paradigm of urbane style. A principal founder of the International Style in the 1920s, Mies is known for his maxim "less is more." Yet the Seagram Building's rich bronze façade, twenty-four-foot-high, marble-clad lobby and custom crafted fittings led one critic to quip, "I've never seen more of less."

Wrapped in fine trappings, the thirty-eight-story shaft of bronze and glass is best known for its powerful and perfectly proportioned form. Like the Lever House, it was an exception to the wedding-cake skyscrapers that stepped back gradually from the street. Mies avoided this formula by setting the entire building back ninety feet from Park Avenue and filling the space with a broad plaza, emphasizing the building's monumental presence.

While the building was created as a monument to the centennial of the distillers Joseph E. Seagram & Company, it could have been one of the mediocre corporate towers that lined Park Avenue in the postwar building boom. The first architect hired

Right: The shaft of bronze and glass has a powerful and perfectly proportioned form.

Left: Designed by Philip Johnson with unerring good taste, the Four Seasons Restaurant on the ground floor is a handsome extension of the Seagram Building's modernist design.

for the job was Charles Luckman, the former president of the Lever Corporation who often got credit for the company's innovative headquarters but, in fact, had little to do with the design. Luckman's proposal for the Seagram site, diagonally across the street from Lever House, would have done little for either building. Fortunately, Phyllis Bronfman Lambert, the daughter of Seagram's owner and an architect herself, was outraged by the undistinguished design, which one critic called "an enormous cigarette lighter," and convinced her father to allow her to replace Luckman with Mies.

In an age of glass and steel skyscrapers, Mies' decision to use bronze was an unusual choice. By making it the dominant material in the curtain wall, the architect seemed to break his own rules. Rather than a transparent skin for the building structure, the curtain wall of bronze framing and bronze-tinted glass is a decorative façade. The fact that it hides structural elements, such as diagonal wind bracings, led architect Louis Kahn to call the building "a beautiful bronze lady in hidden corsets." Yet the geometric precision of the glass and bronze grid acts as an integral part of the tower, reinforcing its rectilinear shape.

The Four Seasons Restaurant, accessible from both the lobby and a side entrance, was also conceived as an extension of the building design. Under Philip Johnson's direction, the restaurant interior, comprised of two beautifully proportioned dining rooms, could only be called lavish minimalism. While he was an early advocate of the International Style in New York, Johnson wanted the restaurant to get away from the sterility that often marked the style. With unerring good taste, he combined unobtrusively handsome furnishings with unique works of art, including pieces by Picasso, Joan Miro, and Jackson Pollock, to create a supremely sophisticated setting.

Like the Lever House, the Seagram Building sacrificed office space for the open space of the plaza. But the Seagram's much larger plaza gives the building added dignity

Right: Seen through the bronze and glass entrance, the lobby is an impressive, twenty-four-foot high space, elegantly clad in marble and bronze.

Far Right: At night, the tower seems to hover above the recessed lobby.

and stature. In contrast to the richness of the bronze façade, the plaza is a spare space furnished only with two large reflecting pools and a few trees. Picasso, Brancusi, and Henry Moore offered to contribute sculpture, but Mies felt these works would detract from the building and the plaza. Even benches were rejected. Nonetheless, New Yorkers have made the place their own, sitting and lying down on the low marble-topped parapets that enclose the space. From time to time, the plaza also becomes a public stage for concerts, temporary art installations, and dance performances.

The combination of tower and plaza was so well received by critics and the public that it led to zoning incentives intended to replicate the design. New regulations adopted in 1961 offer a "plaza bonus," allowing builders to construct taller buildings if they include public open space. However, like the Lever House, the Seagram Building proved to be a poor model for less talented hands. The new zoning led to a rash of huge towers set back from the street and surrounded by uninviting, windswept plazas. Little used by the public, many of these empty spaces became a liability for the owners who then put up gates to keep out vagrants. While the owners profited by the added office space in the taller buildings, the barren plazas robbed city streets of their urban vitality. Urged by civic groups, the city eventually adopted new "contextual" regulations, encouraging lower buildings closer to the street. However, this move also had its critics who complained that the regulations limited architectural individuality and produced boring, blocky buildings. While the debate continues today, the Seagram Building, despite its bad influence, is all the more appreciated as a singular work of art.

Guggenheim Museum

Architect: Frank Lloyd Wright

Built: 1956–1959

Before the Guggenheim Museum was built, New Yorkers had never seen anything remotely like it, certainly not on elegant Fifth Avenue. Unadorned concrete exteriors had shown their bare faces only in the city's industrial backyard, never in its residential front parlor where buildings were properly dressed in marble, granite, limestone, and, at a minimum, basic brick. But concrete was only one of the shocking features. The free-standing spiral form looked like a spinning top in the midst of disapproving, stiff-shouldered neighbors. Only America's most original architect would have conceived of such a building and only the most determined could have succeeded in making it a lasting monument to creative architecture.

While the museum is Frank Lloyd Wright's only major work in New York City, it is nonetheless the best known building by this renowned and prolific architect. Sixteen years from concept to completion, the Guggenheim—the most controversial building ever to rise in New York—took longer to finish than the fourteen-year construction of the Brooklyn Bridge. Wright was seventy-six years old when he was asked to design the museum and nearly ninety-two when he died in

Right: Wright used the ancient Babylonian form of the ziggurat, inverting its pyramid shape and making the museum a building to be seen from the top down. The sculpture on top of the smaller wing, designed by Frank Gehry, was installed in 2002. The slab building was designed by Gwathmey Siegel Associates and built in 1992.

Far Right: A cantilevered ramp spirals around the main gallery, rising seventy-five feet to the roof.

Left: The museum's unadorned concrete exterior was a dramatic exception to the neighboring facades of elegant mansions and apartment houses.

Right: The horizontal base accentuates the spiral form above.

April 1959, just six months short of the museum's opening. During this period, the Guggenheim was only one of an astonishing array of buildings that he designed and, in most cases, saw through construction.

In her 1943 letter inviting Wright to design the museum, Hilla von Rebay, the curator of the Guggenheim art collection and a passionate advocate of abstract art, said, "I need a fighter, a lover of space, an agitator, a tester and a wise man." She could not have found a better man than Wright. Despite his other work, he overcame tremendous obstacles to see the museum built, from a long search for a site and delays caused by rising construction costs to staunch opposition from New York City's bureaucracy and vocal world of art.

Wary of urban congestion, Wright at first preferred a site outside of Manhattan in an undeveloped section of the Bronx where he envisioned a horizontal building like those he had designed on the Midwestern prairie and Arizona desert. But as the search dragged on, he realized that the museum's patron, Solomon Guggenheim, a copper mining magnate, had his heart set on Manhattan. Wright switched his thinking to a vertical structure and by early 1944 came up with the spiral form. When Guggenheim finally acquired the Fifth Avenue site opposite Central Park, Wright welcomed the park's open space as breathing room for the building.

The first cost estimate was 750,000 dollars, but in the postwar building boom, the price of construction soared to two and a half million dollars, putting the project on hold for several years. It suffered a further setback when the eighty-eight-year old Guggenheim died in 1949. Over time, Wright gained the family's approval to proceed, but many other New Yorkers tried to stand in his way in the years to come. City engineers questioned the unusual structure, which did not conform to traditional building codes, and demanded exacting changes. Fifth Avenue landlords and tenants maintained that the radically different design clashed with traditional buildings on the stately residential street. The editors of the *New York Times* made the point more strongly, calling the museum "an oversized and indigestible hot cross bun."

While most people complained about the bold exterior, others found something to dislike in the equally unusual interior, a single large room where paintings were hung on sloping walls along a spiraling ramp. Wright believed that the continuous circular path was a vast improvement over the wandering route in and out of rooms in traditional museums. But artists and art critics felt that the distracting surroundings would overshadow the art it was meant to showcase. This fear reverberated in the art world as soon as the plans were made public. It reached a peak of opposition when the leading abstract artists of the day, including Willem de Kooning and Robert Motherwell, sent the Guggenheim trustees a letter of strong protest. Wright made his usual caustic reply, "...you all know too little of the nature of the mother art—architecture." Compared to architecture, he implied, painting was a mere child. Once the museum was finally completed, however, a new voice on the *New York Times*, Ada Louise Huxtable, praised the "luminous, soaring, unified space...the daring cantilevers, the unorthodox building shapes that add up to a spectacular new architecture of great visual excitement."

Although Wright was not terribly fond of abstract painting, he would no doubt be pleased to see that the museum's place on Fifth Avenue is now beyond reproach. When a ten-story addition was proposed in 1985, the museum was once again the center of controversy, not because something radical had been proposed, but because it might have altered a recognized work of art.

Ford Foundation Building

Architects: Kevin Roche, John Dinkeloo & Associates. Winter Garden, landscape architect Dan Kiley.

Built: 1967

In an era of windowless offices locked into air-conditioned isolation, the Ford Foundation Building was a breath of fresh air. Cradling a glass-enclosed garden in its granite arms, the building turned conventional office construction inside out. Widely regarded as New York City's best building of the 1960s, a lean time for architecture, the building was nonetheless a distinctive achievement. It also was one of the first green sprouts of environmental design.

Only twelve stories high, the building has a ten-story-high skylit atrium lushly filled with full-grown trees and thousands of shrubs, vines, and plants. It is a unique setting for the foundation's employees whose offices overlook the garden court. Architecture critic Ada Louise Huxtable called it "one of the most romantic environments ever devised by corporate man."

Like the Lever Corporation that built a light-filled tower and roof garden for its employees a decade earlier, the Ford Foundation had a humanistic environment in mind for its staff. But the foundation went beyond physical amenities to create a setting for social interaction that complemented its philanthropic goals of supporting third world communities.

Right: Granite and monumental from the outside, the Ford Foundation Building has a green winter garden at its core.

Left: The glass-enclosed atrium affords dramatic views in and out of the building.

Left: Filled with trees and plants, the skylit atrium rises ten stories, nearly the entire height of the building.

Right: Changing light and shadows play on the interior of the atrium.

Kevin Roche, the principal architect, saw the interior garden as a place "to look across the court and see your fellow man or sit on a bench in the garden and discuss the problems of Southeast Asia."

The building design also had a sense of responsibility for the urban community around it. Its relatively low height reflected that of its neighbors. Its materials—brown granite with flecks of orange and pink and an exposed steel frame that has oxidized to a rich, wood-like patina—have a warm tone, unlike the icy chrome and glass of corporate towers. The interior garden, landscaped by the celebrated designer Dan Kiley, is a green oasis to people entering from the street, and was an early method of cooling temperatures and filtering the air. Although the foursquare building has an imposing presence on the street, the large amount of open space reserved for the garden balances the monumental exterior.

However, to critics keenly aware of the Ford Foundation's great wealth, the building seemed like "a temple unto itself" and an extravagant waste of space. Architectural

historian Vincent Scully went so far as to call the atrium a "sultanic garden." But the normally hard-to-please Huxtable, disgusted with what she saw as the era's overbearing commercialism and underachieving design, championed the building as a lesson for the times. "...it is a large potential dose of design quality in a city that matches its extraordinary vitality with the deadliness of its building clichés." Far from a waste, she proclaimed it "a civic gesture of beauty and excellence." Years later, Huxtable's replacement at the *New York Times*, Paul Goldberger, confirmed her belief that the building was an appropriate expression of philanthropy, one that "by its very presence on the streetscape, benefits the entire city."

Avant-garde in the sterile 1960s, interior courts had been used long before the Ford Foundation headquarters and appeared in many buildings that came after it. A number of late-nineteenth century buildings organized offices around an interior skylit court to capture more daylight. In the 1970s and 1980s, the landscaped atrium also became a feature of lavish corporate lobbies and shopping malls. Today, in Midtown Manhattan's world of concrete, glass, and steel, the verdant intimacy of the Ford Foundation's inner core still comes as a rare and unexpected delight.

Citicorp Center

Architects: Hugh Stubbins & Associates, Emery Roth & Sons, and
Gwathmey Siegel & Associates.

Built: 1977

From the corner of Lexington and 53rd, this silver-skinned tower, topped off by its 45-degree-angled roof, looks like a colossal, sharp-beaked bird resting on one enormous leg. Along with three others hidden from this view, the gigantic leg is a "supercolumn" tucked under the fifty-nine-story tower. Each column, ten stories high and twenty-four feet square, stands, not at the four corners of the building, but in the middle of each of its block-long sides. The corners extend seventy-two feet out from each leg, giving the building a precarious appearance.

Although the public would not know all the facts for many years, Citicorp's acrobatic act narrowly escaped an engineering disaster. Ironically, the inspiration for the extraordinary design was, in fact, divine. St. Peter's Lutheran Church, on the site since 1862, gave the builders a moral imperative. The church would be demolished and replaced as part of the Citibank project, but the agreement required that "nothing but free sky" could be above the new, free-standing church. A generous plaza was also required to continue the church's tradition of welcoming the public. Since the bank wanted the building to take up the entire site, the architects consulted an engineering specialist, William LeMessurier. He devised the supercolumn

Far Right: Citicorp's sharply angled roof was a distinctive addition to the New York skyline.

Right: Supported by "supercolumns," the tower from this view appears to be balancing itself on one enormous leg.

scheme to leave room at the site's corners for an unencumbered new church and sunken plaza. LeMessurier added several features to strengthen the building against the force of high winds. Under its aluminum skin, the towering shaft was braced with diagonal trusses on all sides. Its slanted crown enclosed a 400-ton mass of concrete to counter the sway of the building. Known as a tuned mass damper, the concrete mass is a standard feature in very tall buildings today, but Citicorp was the first time it had ever been used.

Despite these precautions, the building had a hidden fault. LeMessurier came upon it by chance in June 1978, a year after the building had been completed, when a question from a student led him to do some checking and recalculating. Although he had called for the diagonal braces to be welded to the building frame, the contractors had bolted them instead. For this unusually configured tower, the change had dire implications. Learning of the substitution after the fact, LeMessurier calculated the impact of hurricane force winds hitting the bolted braces at an angle—a test that had not been conducted before—and discovered the shocking fact that such winds carried a fifty percent chance of toppling the building. Located in Manhattan's densely developed Midtown section, Citicorp was a threat not only to its own tenants but also to thousands of others in the surrounding buildings.

After wind tunnel tests confirmed his fears, LeMessurier notified Citibank's Chairman Walter Wriston who authorized immediate repairs. The engineer's solution was surprisingly simple, welding huge braces over the vulnerable points. The steel bandaids were applied under the cover of

construction scaffolding and once the aluminum façade was replaced, the repairs were permanently hidden from view. While the work was done at night to minimize public fears, Citibank alerted the city's emergency forces who mapped out a potential evacuation plan for ten blocks surrounding the building. By October, just five months after LeMessurier had discovered the threat, the

Left: Looking up at the tower from the sunken plaza.

Right: St. Peter's Church was rebuilt as a distinctive modern building at the base of the tower.

repairs were completed, solving the problem and erasing the fear of disaster. Luckily for Citibank, New York newspapers were on strike during the entire procedure and the story never reached the public. The full details did not come out until 1995 when it became the subject of an article in the *New Yorker* magazine.

In his first thoughts about the building, the architect Hugh Stubbins saw the project as a way to devote "the resources of big business...to humanity." In the world of real estate development, that desire found its expression in an indoor shopping mall, but one unlike any that the city had seen before. Partially underground, the first seven stories of the building were constructed around a skylit atrium and filled with shops, trees, and a vast food hall. Tremendously popular with the public, it transcended its commercial core and became a lively, festive gathering place in an unlikely setting—the bowels of a skyscraper.

Just outside of the commercial cornucopia, the new St. Peter's Church offers sustenance for the soul. Shaped like a prism and set at a 45-degree angle to the street, the church maintains its own identity and also complements the tower above. With not one but two slanted roofs, it points not only to the heavens above but, along the way, to the angled top of Citicorp's crown. Like the church, the tower's distinctive crown had good intentions. Facing south, the slope was designed to be a solar collector to supplement the building's tremendous use of energy. However, tests later revealed that the reduction in cost was not worth the investment in special equipment. All the same, the crown has won its way into New Yorkers' hearts.

Trump Tower

Architects: Der Scutt with Swanke Hayden Connell and landscape architect

Thomas Balsley Associates

Built: 1983

Trump Tower does not have an observation deck or a souvenir shop but it draws hordes of tourists all the same. Filled with upscale shops and deluxe apartments and offices, the tower puts luxury on display. The extravagantly styled building has been a New York City attraction ever since its start in the 1980s real estate boom—a high-rise heyday that rivaled the 1920s skyscraper race for fame.

The sleek tower, one of the first New York skyscrapers to burst out of its glass box, has a taut glass skin pleated in folds over the length of its sixty-eight floors. The lower stories are an inverted pyramid of glass cubes, supporting a small forest of trees. Beneath the exterior, it was the tallest and most expensive reinforced concrete structure of its time. Its six-story atrium, where a waterfall runs down peach-pink marble walls, set the standard for sumptuous lobbies in a period of lavish design.

But it was the personality behind the building that caused the real sensation. In an era known for aggressive developers, the youngest and brashest was Donald Trump, a thirty-something phenomenon who perfected the art of real estate deals and self promotion. The

Far Right: One of the first skyscrapers to burst out of its glass box, Trump Tower has an innovative façade of "pleated" shapes.

Right: Sleek elevators with brass rails and mirrored sides cross the gleaming six-story atrium.

son of a successful developer of middle-class housing in Brooklyn and Queens, Trump learned the business in the far reaches of the city but always had his eye on Manhattan. He had captured the city spotlight in 1980 by transforming the dowager Commodore Hotel next to Grand Central Terminal. Named for "Commodore" Cornelius Vanderbilt, the railroad magnate who had built the terminal, the ailing hotel became the sparkling, glass-enclosed Grand Hyatt. The multi-million dollar project helped pull the city up from its long economic slide in the 1970s and became a shining symbol of reinvestment at the gateway to Midtown Manhattan. But Trump would soon put his own name on a more impressive building.

Glamorous from the outside, Trump Tower had a no-nonsense engineer behind the scenes. Barbara Res had worked on construction of the Grand Hyatt and came to Trump Tower as the first woman engineer in charge of building a skyscraper. Like Trump, she was in her thirties and just as determined as her boss to get the job done. With signs in her office reading, "Sometimes the best man for the job is a woman," she juggled three sets of city building codes for office, retail, and residential development and kept the project moving despite its mounting controversy and criticism.

Critics charged that the glass tower did not belong on this part of Fifth Avenue, a quietly elegant stretch of low-rise, limestone-clad stores. Trump Tower was going to displace the Art Deco

department store, Bonwit Teller, and opponents warned that it would do further harm by clashing with other Fifth Avenue doyens such as Tiffany's and Bergdorf Goodman. But this prime location, in the midst of the city's most famous shopping district, just a block away from the Plaza Hotel and Central Park, was a developer's dream.

Trump had pursued it for years and buying the site in partnership with a major insurance company was the coup of his young career. Brushing off his critics, he brought an impressive collection of international shops to the atrium, along with movie and television stars to live in the luxury condominiums. In what would become his

Left: Like many powerful developers before him, Donald Trump made his building a mark of personal achievement, but did so in his own extravagant style. His name, stamped in gold, is a prominent feature of the tower's Fifth Avenue entrance.

Far Left: The lobby is a sumptuous expanse of peach-pink marble.

signature style, he promoted the building as "the most spectacular complex...the ultimate in quality at the world's finest location."

While Trump was a newcomer to Fifth Avenue, he quickly became a full-fledged member of the city's skyscraper club by turning every square foot of his building to commercial advantage. Working closely with his architect, Der Scutt, he made sure that the sophisticated design had marketing appeal and real estate savvy. The zigzag pleats of glass created interesting interiors with a multitude of windows and views for the 250 condominiums. The glass cube projections became built-in terraces for the thirteen floors of offices below. The atrium shops also had hidden benefits. Since the city wanted to preserve this part of Fifth Avenue as a shopping district, new stores were eligible for zoning incentives, adding up to several more floors for the tower.

Although Trump promoted the building with show business pizzazz, he made good on his promises of high quality. Using the finest materials and expert craftsmen, he made the Trump name a luxury brand, replicating it later in a number of apartment houses in other parts of Manhattan. Even some of his critics, such as Paul Goldberger, who questioned the appropriateness of a glass tower on Fifth Avenue, had only good things to say about the building's details. The atrium's "carefully, cut, sensuous marble...and balustrades of glass and brass...suggest not only a willingness to spend money, but also a knowledge of how to spend it correctly."

Today, Fifth Avenue's elegant shops are none the worse for their towering neighbor, nor for the latest newcomers, the showcase stores of Nike and the Walt Disney Company. With its polished gold trim, lustrous marble, and gleaming glass, Trump Tower has joined Tiffany's and Bergdorf's as a classy member of the older generation.

New 42nd Street Studios

Architects: Platt, Byard, Dovell, lighting design. Anne Miletello, vortex lighting.

Built: 2000

Racing through the heart of Midtown Manhattan, 42nd Street is the pulse of the city. A century ago, it was still the city's outskirts, but it quickened with development as Grand Central Terminal, the Chrysler Building, United Nations, and many other buildings rose up along its eastern end. Passing west through Times Square, the street flashed with the marquees of Broadway theaters. In the first half of the century, these lights burned so brightly that the name itself, 42nd Street, became synonymous with the city's famous theater district. But by the 1970s, the block that once was the center of the district, 42nd Street between Broadway and Eighth Avenue—the heart of Times Square—had become the most notoriously squalid strip in the city. The marquees that once displayed the biggest names on Broadway now boasted "Best Porn XXX in Town."

Plagued by drug dealers and sex shops, the block gave the entire street a bad name.

Reborn in the 1990s as the "New 42nd Street," the block shines brighter than ever before with elegantly refurbished theaters and glittering new attractions. In 2000, it added an architectural gem, the New 42nd Street Studios, a small structure that brought a big

· **Far Right:** Colored lights wash over stainless steel louvers on the front of the building, creating a sophisticated version of a Times Square marquee. A translucent light screen on the lower left corner of the façade marks a small theater on the ground floor.

Right: Orchestrated by computers, the light show on the façade has 500 ever-changing patterns.

Left: The studio space, used by small dance and theater companies, provides dramatic views of the Times Square area.

Below Right: The top-floor terrace offers a view of an avant-garde building of an earlier age, the 1931 McGraw-Hill Building in the far left background.

Below Far Right: At night, the studios are bathed in the light show playing on the façade.

change to building design. Like the theater district itself, the new building is all lights and action. The block has been cleaned up but it is far from boring. In keeping with the Times Square tradition of flashing billboards, new buildings in the theater district are required to include bold electric signs on their facades. In doing so, the architects for the New 42nd Street Studios reinvented the glass curtain wall of postwar design into a twenty-first-century light show. Even more surprising, they did it without a word of advertisement. Every night, the front of the ten-story building puts on quite a performance. The building has a high-tech grid of stainless steel louvers across its glass façade. Lights below the louvers and along the length of the building reflect off the grid and glass, creating a changing rainbow of pulsating color across the entire facade. Orchestrated by computers, the show is mesmerizing and never quite the same.

The block is jammed with other attractions that vie for attention. Smack in the middle, right across the street from a Walt Disney theater and a Madame Tussaud Wax Museum, the studio building does its own thing with sophisticated style and perfect execution. Joseph Giovannini, architecture critic for *New York* magazine, says the building "changes the state of architecture from solid to liquid," breaking new ground with abstract, translucent, continuously changing patterns of light.

Yet the façade is not just for show. Light is an integral part of the design and the building's form exactly fits its function. It was built for the New 42nd Street Inc., the nonprofit organization that led the revitalization of the street over the past decade, managing the restoration of seven historic theaters. Ironically, as the area improved and as city real estate values in general increased in the 1990s, many dance and theater companies were squeezed out of their studios by rising rents. Cora Cahan, the nonprofit's president and a former dancer, recognized the need "to claim a place for artists on 42nd Street where the art of creation could take place." The organization raised funds to construct the building and provide studios to small companies at affordable rents. Previously making do in shabby quarters, dancers, actors, and musicians now enjoy fourteen state-of-the-art studios. A small theater occupies the ground floor and offices for the nonprofit and performance companies are on the top.

Charles Platt, a principal architect for the project, conceived the building as a "factory for the arts." Similar to industrial lofts, the studios have high ceilings and even bigger than usual factory windows. Wrapped in glass, the large rooms afford maximum daylight and great views—both in and out. During rehearsals, passersby on the street can enjoy views of the working artists. At night, the light show playing on the building is also in constant motion. "The shimmering, ever-changing exterior," Cahan says, "is a symbol of the experimentation and vibrancy within."

Rose Center for Earth and Space

Architect: Polshek Partnership

Built: 2000

Holden Caulfield always liked the Museum of Natural History simply because it never seemed to change. For the troubled protagonist of *The Catcher in the Rye*, the cavernous museum and its musty displays offered comforting stability in his turbulent adolescent life. But if Holden came to the museum today, its new wing would rock his world.

The Rose Center for Earth and Space has broken out of its Victorian home with a design that crosses new frontiers in time, space, and technology. Nearly a century ago, the visionary architect Le Corbusier said that the history of architecture is the history of the window. Arriving at the dawn of the new millennium, the Rose Center is all window.

The six-story-high glass cube is the largest and finest example of a glass curtain wall ever built in the nation. Perfectly transparent, it holds a ninety-foot-diameter sphere, the replacement

Above: The entrance to the planetarium beckons like a waiting space ship.

Right: Like the sky itself, the museum's new planetarium gives off a blue glow at night.

for the red brick Hayden Planetarium. Built in 1935, the old Art Deco structure at the north end of the museum was a dark, cozy haunt for many Holden Caulfields growing up in the city. The new building, emanating a silver sheen by day and a blue glow by night, has left jaws dropping across the city.

Its creator, New York-based architect, James Polshek, calls it a "cosmic cathedral," inspiring visitors with the wonders of the universe "in much the same way that the monumental spaces of medieval cathedrals inspired visiting pilgrims." While the stained-glass windows of cathedrals convey the spiritualism of religion, Polshek used the latest glass technology to express the clarity of modern science.

The cube comprises of 736 individual panes of "water white" glass. Their crystal clarity was achieved by reducing the amount of iron in the glass. Nearly invisible stainless steel rods and spider web-like fittings hold the panes, making them look like a single sheet of glass. Free of interior columns, which would have obstructed the sphere, the cube is supported by an ingenious system of trusses held in place along the roof and walls by tension. The 2000-ton sphere, surrounded by scale models of planets and stars, seems to float within the cube, but it is actually held up by tapered steel legs. While early skyscrapers like the Chrysler Building evoke images of rocket

Left: Entrance to the sphere's Big Bang Theater. Below is the Cosmic Pathway, an illuminated ramp encircling the sphere.

Right: Scale models of the planets surround the ninety-foot-diameter sphere. This view also shows the steel trusses that support the six-story-high glass walls by tension.

ships, the huge sphere is an updated version of a spaceship with its landing gear down, ready to carry the public up into the universe.

A trip through the new center is a fascinating journey into space. Architect Michael Crosbie has observed that walking across the lobby floor, polished black stone twinkling with glass parti-cles, is "like walking across the night sky." On the main floor, video screens blink and beep with interactive displays. (Today's Holden Caulfields are computer whizzes and feel right at home.) The sphere looms as large as an approaching planet, beckoning for the journey to begin. As in the Guggenheim Museum, the building is best seen from the top down. Ascending an elevator to the crown of the sphere, one enters the Sky Theater for a flight through the galaxy via the world's largest virtual reality simulator and most impressive sound system in the city. The Big Bang Theater on the sphere's lower level provides an inside view of the origin of the universe. The return to earth is along the Cosmic Pathway, a 360-foot-long illuminated ramp that encircles the sphere and flashes with scenes of distant galaxies. One can look into the far reaches of the uni-verse and, at the same time, marvel at immediate and changing perspectives of the sphere, the cube, and the city beyond.

Six years in the making, the 210-million-dollar Rose Center reflects not only the universe but also the civic aspirations and great resources of New York City. The innovative design and tech-nology are a dramatic departure from the Beaux-Arts buildings of the city's past, notably the stately main section of the Natural History Museum itself, as well as the classic temples of the New York Public Library and Metropolitan Museum. But the futuristic Rose Center is squarely within the noble tradition of these and other great buildings. Uniting its goals with its architecture, it serves and inspires the public in a building unique to its time.

Index